Start TO Finish
Second Series

Everyday Products

FROM Sheep TO Sweater

ROBIN NELSON

 LERNER PUBLICATIONS COMPANY ▶ Minneapolis

Lerner Publications Company
A division of Lerner Publishing Group, Inc.
241 First Avenue North
Minneapolis, MN 55401 U.S.A.

Website address: www.lernerbooks.com

Photo Acknowledgments
The images in this book are used with the permission of: © Isselee/Dreamstime.com, p. 1; © Juice Images, p. 3; © Monty Rakusen/Cultura/Getty Images, p. 5; © iStockphoto.com/Berna Namoglu, p. 7; © Joerg Boethling/Alamy, p. 9; © John T. Fowler/Alamy, p. 11; © Guy Croft Industrial/Alamy, pp. 13, 15; © Kevin Foy/Alamy, p. 17; © ColorBlind Images/Blend Images/Getty Images, p. 19; © iStockphoto.com/Antagain, p. 21; © Ariel Skelley/Blend Images/Getty Images, p. 23.

Front cover: © Jeffrey Van Daele/Dreamstime.com.

Main body text set in Arta Std Book 20/26.
Typeface provided by International Typeface Corp.

Library of Congress Cataloging-in-Publication Data

Nelson, Robin, 1971–
    From sheep to sweater / by Robin Nelson.
        p.   cm. — (Start to finish, second series.
    Everyday products)
    Includes index.
    ISBN 978–0–7613–6564–8 (lib. bdg. : alk. paper)
    1. Woolen and worsted manufacture—Juvenile
literature. I. Title.
TS1626.N45 2013
677'.31—dc23   2012008477

Manufactured in the United States of America
1 – MG – 12/31/12

TABLE OF Contents

A ſweater keeps me warm. How is it made?

3

Sheep are raised on farms or ranches.

A farmer raises sheep. The farmer feeds the sheep every day. The sheep eat a mixture of hay, grass, and grains. This food helps the sheep to grow thick, healthy coats of **wool**.

The coats are clipped.

In the spring, the sheep's coats are clipped. This is called **shearing**. A person shears each sheep's wool off in one big piece called a **fleece**. The sheep will grow another coat over the summer to keep it warm in the winter.

The wool is sorted.

Workers sort the wool. They remove wool that is dark or dirty. They keep thick wool that is light in color.

The wool is washed and dried.

Workers wash the wool many times.
Washing removes bugs, straw, and mud
from the wool. Then the wool is dried.

The wool is combed.

Workers or machines comb the wool to remove knots. This is called **carding**. Carding makes the wool soft.

The yarn is spun.

A spinning wheel twists the wool.
The wool forms long pieces of yarn.

The yarn is dyed.

The yarn is still the color of a sheep. The yarn must be dyed to change its color. A worker dips the wool into a colored liquid to dye it. Yarn can be dyed any color of the rainbow.

Shoppers buy the yarn.

Trucks take the yarn to stores. People
go to a store to buy yarn. This woman
picks out blue and pink yarn.

A sweater is made.

One way of turning yarn into a sweater is by **knitting**. A knitter uses two long needles to make loops and knots with the yarn. The yarn is knitted into the shape of a sweater.

I wear my new sweater!

The wool in my sweater used to keep a sheep warm. Now it keeps me warm!

Glossary

carding (KAR-ding): combing wool

dyed (DYD): dipped in colored liquid

fleece (FLEES): a sheep's wool after it is clipped

knitting (NIHT-ing): using needles to make yarn into a sweater

shearing (SHEER-ing): clipping a sheep's wool

wool (WUL): the soft, curly coat of a sheep

Index